First World War
and Army of Occupation
War Diary
France, Belgium and Germany

40 DIVISION
Divisional Troops
Machine Gun Corps
40 Battalion
25 February 1918 - 10 May 1918

WO95/2601/5

The Naval & Military Press Ltd
www.nmarchive.com
Published in association with The National Archives

Published by

The Naval & Military Press Ltd

Unit 10 Ridgewood Industrial Park,

Uckfield, East Sussex,

TN22 5QE England

Tel: +44 (0) 1825 749494

www.naval-military-press.com

www.nmarchive.com

This diary has been reprinted in facsimile from the original. Any imperfections are inevitably reproduced and the quality may fall short of modern type and cartographic standards.

© **Crown Copyright**
Images reproduced by permission of The National Archives, London, England, 2015.

Contents

Document type	Place/Title	Date From	Date To
Miscellaneous	WO95/2601/5		
Heading	40 Div Troops 40 Bn Machine Gun Corps 1918 Mar-1918 May		
War Diary	Enniskillen Camp (Ervillers)	25/02/1918	27/02/1918
War Diary	Armagh Camp Hamelincourt	28/02/1918	28/02/1918
Heading	40th Battalion Machine Gun Corps March 1918		
War Diary	Lens 11 Hamlincourt (Armagh Camp)	01/03/1918	02/03/1918
War Diary	Blaireville	03/03/1918	09/03/1918
War Diary	Lens 11 Blaireville	10/03/1918	11/03/1918
War Diary	Beaurains	12/03/1918	16/03/1918
War Diary	Lens 11 "Beaurains"	17/03/1918	21/03/1918
War Diary	Hamelincourt	22/03/1918	22/03/1918
War Diary	Lens 11 Hamelincourt	22/03/1918	22/03/1918
War Diary	Ayette	23/03/1918	24/03/1918
War Diary	Monchy-Au-Bois	25/03/1918	26/03/1918
War Diary	Beaudricourt	27/03/1918	28/03/1918
War Diary	La Thieuloye	29/03/1918	29/03/1918
War Diary	Lens 11 La Thieuloye	30/03/1918	30/03/1918
War Diary	La Thieuloye Sailly Sur Lys (Hazebrouck 5a)	31/03/1918	31/03/1918
Miscellaneous	40th. Battalion Machine Gun Corps. Appendix 1.		
Miscellaneous	40th. Battalion Machine Gun Corps.	26/03/1918	26/03/1918
Miscellaneous	40th. Battalion Machine Gun Corps. Casualties Officers.		
Miscellaneous	40th. Battalion Machine Gun Corps	28/03/1918	28/03/1918
Heading	40th Battalion Machine Gun Corps April 1918		
Heading	40th Battalion Machine Gun Corps. War Diary April 1918.		
War Diary	Hazebrouck 5 A. Sailly-sur Lys	01/04/1918	01/04/1918
War Diary	Croix Du Bac	02/04/1918	08/04/1918
War Diary	Hazebrouck 5 A.	09/04/1918	10/04/1918
War Diary	La Haute Loge	11/04/1918	15/04/1918
War Diary	Moulle	16/04/1918	18/04/1918
War Diary	Hazebrouck 5 A. Moulle	19/04/1918	21/04/1918
War Diary	Moringhem	22/04/1918	29/04/1918
War Diary	Hazebrouck 5 A. St Omer	30/04/1918	30/04/1918
Miscellaneous	40th. Battalion Machine Gun Corps.	16/04/1918	16/04/1918
Miscellaneous	40th. Battalion Machine Gun Corps.	23/04/1918	23/04/1918
Miscellaneous	40th. Battalion Machine Gun Corps.		
Map	Croix Du Bac.		
Map			
Heading	40th. Battalion Machine Gun Corps. War Diary For Month Of May 1918.		
War Diary	Hazebrouck 5a. St Omer	01/05/1918	10/05/1918

woas/2601/5

40 DIV TROOPS

40 BN MACHINE GUN CORPS

1918 MAR — 1918 MAY

40th Batt. M.G. Corps.

40 Bn. M.G. Corps

Army Form C. 2118.

WAR DIARY
or
INTELLIGENCE SUMMARY.
(Erase heading not required.)

Instructions regarding War Diaries and Intelligence Summaries are contained in F. S. Regs., Part II. and the Staff Manual respectively. Title pages will be prepared in manuscript.

Place	Date	Hour	Summary of Events and Information	Remarks and references to Appendices
ENNISKILLEN CAMP. (ERVILLERS)	25/2/18		Formation of Battalion under O.B./407 Q dated 19.2.18. and 40th Division No. C/119/A at 9.a.m. Dispositions as follows. Battalion Headquarters and 120th. Machine Gun Company at ENNISKILLEN CAMP ERVILLERS. 119th. Machine Gun Company at NEUVILLE VITASSE, 121st Machine Gun Company at DURHAM CAMP B. BOISLEUX. 244th. Machine Gun Company DURBOW CAMP, MORY.	Copy of Operation Order Attached.
ENNISKILLEN CAMP. (ERVILLERS)	26/2/18		Inter Company relief.	
ENNISKILLEN CAMP. (ERVILLERS)	27/2/18		Companies and Battalion Headquarters as above.	
ARMAGH CAMP HAMELINCOURT.	28/2/18		Battalion Headquarters and 119th. Machine Gun Company move to ARMAGH CAMP, HAMELINCOURT.	

McCafee
Lt. Col.
C.O. 40th Batt. M.G. Corps
5/2/8

40th Divisional M.G.C.

WAR DIARY

40th BATTALION

MACHINE GUN CORPS

MARCH 1918

Report on Operations 21st-26th March 1918.

Army Form C. 2118.

WAR DIARY
or
INTELLIGENCE SUMMARY.

40 M.G.Bn.
March 1918

(Erase heading not required.)

Instructions regarding War Diaries and Intelligence Summaries are contained in F.S. Regs., Part II. and the Staff Manual respectively. Title pages will be prepared in manuscript.

Place	Date	Hour	Summary of Events and Information	Remarks and references to Appendices
LENS 11 HAMINCOURT (ARLAGH CAMP)	March 1st.		Headquarters and A Company and D Company at HAMINCOURT. "B" Company at NEUVILLE VITTASSE attached to 3rd. Battalion Machine Gun Corps. "C" Company at LORY, attached to 59th. Battalion Machine Gun Corps, these two Companies were in support positions, "A" and "D" Companies training. Order No. 3, issued for move and concentration of Battalion at BLAIREVILLE. "B" and "C" Companies to be withdrawn from the 3rd. and 59th. Battalion Machine Gun Corps respectively. Received instructions re entrainment whilst in G.H.Q. Reserve from the 119th and 121st. Brigades.	
	March 2nd.		General preparations for move. Issued amendment to Order No. 3.; "C" Company to remain with 59th. Battalion Machine Gun Corps until 8.p.m. 3rd. instant. Additional instructions received from 121st. Brigade re entrainment whilst in G.H.Q. Reserve.	
BLAIREVILLE	March 3rd.		Move of Headquarters, "A", "B" and "D" Companies to BLAIREVILLE complete.	
	March 4th.		"C" Company joined about 1.a.m. Battalion training commenced, recreational training in the afternoon. Further instructions received from 121st. Brigade re entraining whilst in G.H.Q. Reserve. Instructions received from 40th. Division and 120th. Brigade re entraining whilst in G.H.Q. Reserve. Battalion to be prepared to move at 24 hours notice, whilst in G.H.Q.Reserve.	
	March 5th.		Training - arrangements made for all ranks to visit Tank Depot at WAILLY. Lecture was given by Major COULON A.G.S., 3rd ARMY on Bayonet Fighting and Recreational Training.	
	March 6th.		Training - "A" and "B" Companies engaged in a tactical exercise with 119th. Brigade.	
	March 7th.		Training - Lecture given by G.S.O.ll on Discipline. Orders received from 40th.Division Re in the event of an attack taking place on the front of the VI Corps or of the left Division of the VI Corps or right Division of the XVII Corps.	
	March 8th.		Training - Battalion was inspected by Lieut.General HALDANE, VI Corps Commander. Battalion played Rugby against 13th. EAST SURREYS, result 32 to 0 in our favour.	
	March 9th.		Training - "C" and "D" Companies took part in a tactical exercise with 121st. Brigade.	

Army Form C. 2118.

WAR DIARY
or
INTELLIGENCE SUMMARY.
(Erase heading not required.)

Instructions regarding War Diaries and Intelligence Summaries are contained in F. S. Regs., Part II and the Staff Manual respectively. Title pages will be prepared in manuscript.

Place	Date	Hour	Summary of Events and Information	Remarks and references to Appendices
LENS 11.March BLAIREVILLE	March 10th.		Church services were held for all denominations. Played Rugby in the afternoon against 18th. WELSH, result 3 - 3. Issued order No.4, instructions to Companies whilst in G.H.Q. Reserve. "A" Company with 119th. Brigade Group, Headquarters, "B" and "D" Companies with 120th.Brigade Group, "C" Company with 121st. Brigade Group. Received order - Division held in readiness to move at 12 hours notice at 5.p.m.	
	March 11th.		From information received it appears probable that the enemy will launch an attack on the VI Corps front on the morning of the 13th. MARCH. Headquarters and Companies warned to move to BOISLEAUX Area on the 12th MARCH. Battalion re-distributed as follows :- Headquarters, "A" and "C" Companies with 119th. Brigade Group, "B" and "D" with 120th. Brigade Group. Companies for purposes of command grouped as follows :- "A" and "C" Companies will form the Left Wing and will be under the command of Capt. D.J.AMERY-PARKES, "B" and "D" Companies will form the Right Wing and will be under the command of Capt. M.C.COOPER. Issued Order No 6 dealing with this.	
"BEAURAINS"	March 12th.		Move to BOISLEAUX Area complete by 9.p.m. Headquarters, "A" and "C" Companies established at CARLISLE CAMP, near BEAURAINS. "B" Company at ERVILLERS - "D" Company at HAMLINCOURT. All units ordered to hold themselves whilst in close reserve to move at 3 hours notice from 8.a.m. to 8.p.m. and 1½ hours notice from 8.p.m. to 8.a.m.	
	March 13th.		Situation normal. Commanding Officer visited 34th and 3rd Battalions Machine Gun Corps in the line. Company Commanders reconnoitred Corps and Army lines. Received instruction from 40th. Division re entraining station whilst in BOISLEAUX Area.	
	March 14th.		Issued instructions re entraining whilst in the "BOISLEAUX" Area for the purpose of a move Companies to be grouped as follows :- 119th Brigade Group, "A" Company - 120th. Brigade Group, Headquarters, "B" and "D" Companies - 121st. Brigade Group, C Company.	
	March 15th.		Order to be prepared to move received 6.30.a.m. Ready to move reported at 7.45.a.m. this was a trial to find out the preparedness of units. Message received at 4.a.m. that deserter states that enemy is going to attack opposite MONCHY on the morning of the 18th instant.	
	March 16th.		Issued instructions to all officers and N.C.Os. who are to reconnoitre daily the 3rd System of the VI Corps front.	

Army Form C. 2118.

WAR DIARY
or
INTELLIGENCE SUMMARY.
(Erase heading not required.)

Instructions regarding War Diaries and Intelligence Summaries are contained in F.S. Regs, Part II. and the Staff Manual respectively. Title pages will be prepared in manuscript.

Place	Date	Hour	Summary of Events and Information	Remarks and references to Appendices
LENS 11. "BEAURAINS"	March 17th.		Instructions received from 40th. Division for move of Brigade Groups to positions of Assembly in the event of an attack taking place on the VI and XVII Corps fronts.	
	March 18th.		Amendment to Order No 5 issued detailing moves to positions of Assembly. Situation normal - no enemy attack.	
	March 19th.		Received 40th. Division Order forecasting relief of 3rd. Division on the Left Sector of the VI Corps front by this Division.	
	March 20th.		Issued provisional relief Order No 8 to relieve 3rd Battalion Machine Gun Corps. Orders received for the Battalion to hold itself in readiness to move at ½ an hours notice.	
	March 21st.	5.a.m.	Very heavy bombardment on the whole of the front opened at 5.a.m. Received message from 40th. Division at 6.a.m. to take precautionary measures- message received from 40th. Division at 10.a.m. -"No Infantry attack yet reported".	
		6.30.a.m.	"B" and "D" Companies report ready to move.	
		noon.	40th. Division report BULLECOURT taken. Enemy threatening right flank of 59th. Division. The following moves to take place at once. 120th. Brigade to move to the 3rd System, 121st Brigade to move from BLAIREVILLE to HAMELINCOURT. At 5.p.m. Battalion Headquarters moved to HAMELINCOURT where Divisional Headquarters were now located, "A" and "C" Companies ordered to move to HENIN with the 119th. Brigade.	
		11.30.p.m.	119th Brigade ordered to withdraw from HENIN and occupy the SENSEE Switch. "A" Company to remain on HENIN HILL and come under the orders of G.O.C. 10th Brigade. "C" Company to move with the 119th. Brigade "B" and "D" Companys ordered to take up positions in the 3rd System to support the 120th and 121st Brigades.	
HAMELINCOURT	March 22nd.	6.50.a.m.	O/C "A" Company reports hostile bombardment commenced about 6.20.a.m. on HENIN HILL, he also reports, he has been ordered to send down a Section to the Southern exits of CROISELLES.	
		3.p.m.	Battalion Headquarters moved to AYETTE, Commanding Officer with 40th. Divisional Headquarters moved to BUCQUOY from HAMELINCOURT about 8.p.m. Commanding Officer went round line in the morning (10.a.m.) to ascertain the situation and co-ordinated the Machine Gun Defence of the line. About 2.p.m. information received from O/C "A" Company that at 11s.m. his guns were all in action on HENIN HILL and that the infantry had apparently retired on both flanks. Later mess age states " i have been up to find out the situation, I have 9 guns left. They are all in action.	

Army Form C. 2118.

WAR DIARY
or
INTELLIGENCE SUMMARY.
(Erase heading not required.)

Instructions regarding War Diaries and Intelligence Summaries are contained in F. S. Regs., Part II. and the Staff Manual respectively. Title pages will be prepared in manuscript.

Place	Date	Hour	Summary of Events and Information	Remarks and references to Appendices
LENS 11 HAMELINCOURT	March 22nd.		No Infantry anywhere near them and our own artillery are shelling them ". These guns remained in action till dark, when with the exception of 4 guns on the extreme left they were rushed by the enemy. Three guns with the remnants of their teams succeeded in rejoining Company Headquarters during the night.	
AYETTE.	March 23rd.		At 4.a.m. O/C "A" Company ordered to report by G.O.C. 101st Brigade to Battalion Headquarters Message of congratulation on the splendid defence by the Division, received from Corps Commander. At about 3.P.M. orders for a withdrawal of our right flank to conform with the line of the Right Division were received. Commanding Officer at Headquarters of 119th and 120th Infantry Brigade during night 23/24th. MARCH.	
	March 24th.		Enemy attacks continue all along the 40th. Divisional Front. A Section of "A" Company reported still fighting near NEUVILLE VITTASSE, orders received from VI Corps to withdraw this Section-which was carried out. Orders received for relief of 40th. Division. Battalion to be relieved on the night of the 25th-26th MARCH. Issued orders to "B", "C" and "D" Companies for relief	
MONCHY-AU-BOIS.	March 25th.		Battalion Headquarters and "A" Company moved to MONCHY-AU-BOIS. "B", "C" and "D" Companies joined from the line during the night.	
	March 26th.		Battalion paraded to move to BIENVILLERS-AU-BOIS. Stopped on route and ordered to send guns for the defence of ADINFER WOOD.- BIENVILLERS - Ordered to move to HABARCQ AREA, moved off at mid-night.	
BEAUDRICOURT	March 27th.		On reaching MONCHIET en route for HABARCQ information received that Battalion was to move to BEAUDRICOURT. After a short rest and a meal this was carried out.	
	March 28th.		No movement. Cleaned and rested. Orders received to move to MONCHY BRETON on Division being transferred from 3rd. to 1st. Army.	
LA THIEULOYE	March 29th.		Moved by march to LA THIEULOYE, Medical cases by bus to TINCQUES thence by march route. Warning Order that Division was being transferred from XIIIth Corps to XV Corps with a view to relief of 57th. Division.	

Army Form C. 2118.

WAR DIARY
or
INTELLIGENCE SUMMARY.

(Erase heading not required.)

Instructions regarding War Diaries and Intelligence Summaries are contained in F. S. Regs. Part II. and the Staff Manual respectively. Title pages will be prepared in manuscript.

Place	Date	Hour	Summary of Events and Information	Remarks and references to Appendices
LENS 11 LA THIEULOYE	March 30th.		"B" Company moved by bus with 120th. Brigade Group to SAILLY. Transport by march route, staging at LILLERS.	
LA THIEULOYE SAILLY SUR LYS (HAZEBROUCK 5a.)	March 31st.		Headquarters, "A", "B" and "C" Companies moved by lorry to SAILLY. Transport by march route, staging at LILLERS. Arrangements for relief made between O/C 40th. and 57th. Machine Gun Battalions. "B" and "D" Companies relieved a Company of the 57th Battalion in Right Sector of the line of the FLEURBAIX Sector. 1st Portuguese Division on Right.	
			DETAILED REPORT OF OPERATIONS 21st.- 26th MARCH 1918.	Appendix A.
			CASUALTY REPORT	Appendix B.

40th. BATTALION MACHINE GUN CORPS.

APPENDIX 1.

RECIPIENTS PRESENT AT CERIMONIAL PARADE.

```
No. 27690 Sgt.(A/C.S.M.) Brennan C.
    9051  Cpl. Brown        W.
    26659 L/Cpl.Tasker      J.
    63491 Pte.Daulby        H.
    31004  "   McInnes      J.
    25728 Cpl.Norton        J.
    37482 Pte Tracey        J.
    53634  "  Wilkin        T.
    97988 Cpl Schofield     S.
    82442 Pte(A/Cpl) Wallace W.
    98924 Cpl Hilson        G.
    27585 Pte (L/Cpl) Brook H.
```

RECIPIENTS   CASUALTIES.

```
    46292 Sgt.Read           B.H.
    68452 L/Cpl Little       H.
    16061 Cpl(A/L/Sgt) Porter F.W.
    88173 Pte Howarth        H.
    60407 Sgt Powell         H.W.
    7360  Cpl Tams           J.
    22294 Sgt Mackrell       A.E.
    121780 Cpl.Day           S.G.
    29053 Sgt.McQueen        W.R.
    98930 Cpl.McNeish        J.
    128059 Pte Pigg          A.E.
```

RECIPIENT WITH 33rd BATTALION M.G.CORPS.

```
    10719 Pte McFee         J.K.
```

40th. BATTALION MACHINE GUN CORPS.

AMENDMENT TO CASUALTY REPORT.

PREVIOUSLY REPORTED "MISSING" now
BELIEVED PRISONER OF WAR.

2nd. Lieut. E. LIGHT   26.3.1918.

PREVIOUSLY REPORTED "MISSING" now
REPORTED N.Y.D.GAS by 93rd.Field Ambulance.

No. 30239 Pte. White A.

PREVIOUSLY REPORTED "MISSING" now
REJOINED BATTALION.

No. 16890 Pte. Cheetham J.   (13th. Yorks)
    28246 "   T.C.Davies   18. Welsh

NOT PREVIOUSLY REPORTED now
REPORTED "MISSING"

No. 12170 Corporal Day G.E.R.
    86111 Private Bromley R.E. (20th. Middlesex).
    119248   "   Cockroft
    20066   "   Waters   H.

40th. BATTALION MACHINE GUN CORPS.

CASUALTIES OFFICERS.

40th. Battalion Machine Gun Corps.	A/Major J.H.Oliver Thompson	Killed	21.3.1918.
	A/Captain A.H.Graves	Killed	22.3.1918.
-do-	Lieut. G.E.A.Anderton	Killed	22.3.1918.
-do-	Lieut. A.Duncan.	Killed	25.3.1918.
-do-	2nd.Lieut. S.G.Whitaker	Killed	22.3.1918.
-do-	A/Major S.G.Davey	Missing believed Killed	25.3.1918.
-do-	2nd. Lt. C.E.Amos	Missing believed Killed	25.3.1918.
-do-	2nd. Lieut. W.F.Amsden	Wounded	22.3.1918.
-do-	2nd. Lieut. H.W.Spurrell	Wounded	22.3.1918.
-do-	2nd. Lieut. W.J.Westwood	Wounded	22.3.1918.
-do-	Lieut. R.R.Flood	Wounded	26.3.1918
-do-	2nd. Lieut. J.G.Thomas	Wounded	22.3.1918.
-do-	2nd. Lieut. J. Gordon	Missing	22.3.1918.
-do-	2nd. Lieut. E. Light	Missing	26.3.1918.
-do-	2nd. Lieut. B. Howard	Missing	24.3.1918.
-do-	A/Captain E.F.Phillips	Wounded (Gas)	25.3.1918.
-do-	2nd. Lieut. C.F.L.de Pelham	Wounded (Gas)	25.3.1918.
-do-	2nd. Lieut. W.I.Thams	Slightly Wounded and remained at duty.	21.3.1918.

CASUALTIES OTHER RANKS.

KILLED.

A Company.	No. 29344	Sergeant	Timms	J.W.	
	30251	L/Cpl.	Read	A.	
	60252	Private	Wood	E.	
	29348	"	Dainty	G.A.	
	41486	"	Saunders	A.	(Middlesex)
B Company.	30228	Corporal	Henty	A.J.	
C Company.	29026	Private	Ash	S.	
	29085	L/Cpl.	Powell	C.	
	7699	Corporal	Daley	J.	

DIED OF WOUNDS.

A Company.	3375	Private	Young	H.	(Middlesex)

Casualties continued. (2)

CASUALTIES   OTHER RANKS.

WOUNDED.

A Company.
29053	Sergeant	Mc.Queen	W.R.
81993	Corporal	Fraser	J.
46689	"	Hodges	E.L.
4761	L/Cpl.	Stinton	T.A.
12428	"	Smith	T.H.
24784	private	Hoyle	F.
36349	"	Burgin	A.
125512	"	Hawkins	D.A.
68124	"	Burnard	E.
72899	"	Roberts	J.
127163	"	Wroe	J.R.
26101	"	Russell	A.E.
119203	"	Woodside	J.
99573	"	Johnstone	J.
119202	"	Wales	R.

ATTACHED MEN WOUNDED.
43357	Private	James		(20th. Middlesex)
28859	"	Boon	D	(18th. Welsh)
40749	"	Wigley	L.	(10/11th.H.L.I.)
28484	"	Lawley	W.J.	(18th. Welsh)

B Company.
28444	"	Fleming	J.
5953	"	Taylor	J.
127993	"	Russell	F.
39422	"	McDonald	F.
125144	"	Smith	W.
28539	"	Kirkwood	G.
40874	"	Gill	T.
12549	C.S.M.	Redman	
63923	Sergeant	Barclay	W.A.B.
30204	"	Tremain	J.G.
37266	"	Hampson	W.
30234	Private	Pryke	F.J.

C Company.
45283	Sergeant	Thristian	O.
43197	Corporal	Drake	R.H.
29041	L/Cpl	Maher	P.
63886	"	Lintott	W.
128225	private	Barlow	G.A.
3377	"	Crux	H.W.
16890	"	Hearold	A.
18473	"	Hussey	A.
25703	"	Mugford	A.E.
85439	"	Moore	W.
128255	"	Williams	A.

D Company.
20878	Sergeant	Searle	S.T.
98927	Corporal	Lane	W.
59792	"	Gibbs	F.J.
98925	"	Hunter	W.
119971	L/Cpl.	Fleetcroft	J.S.
119451	private	Balfour	W.J.
119456	"	Bennett	J.H.
98921	"	Craig	J.
123470	"	Jones	G.
123328	"	Jarrett	W.
99626	"	Ross	J.
29244	"	Duncan	W.
20569	"	Evans	W.

WOUNDED and MISSING.

A Company.
119203	Private	Dickie	J.
36415	"	McGarry	R.

C Company.
12118	"	Lynch	A.
128170	"	Marlow	J.

Casualties continued. (3)

CASUALTIES OTHER RANKS.

C Company. WOUNDED. SHELL SHOCK.

No 66700 Private Felshead T.

B Company.
    8641 " Hendry T.
    70211 " Thomas G.

D Company.
    16061 Corporal Porter F.W.

WOUNDED GAS.

B Company.
    123584 Private Fearon J.

WOUNDED and PRISONER.

C Company.
    25702 L/Cpl. Goggin R.
    85111 Private Warren W.

WOUNDED REMAINED AT DUTY.

A Company.
    46292 Sergeant Read B.H.

MISSING.

A Company.
    72880 Private Evans T.J.
    118996 " Fraser G.
    68181 " Ashworth A.
    85588 " Crombie T.
    105504 " Smith E.W.
    115825 " Carter F.W.
    72893 " Fox I.
    43727 " Nunn A.
    127492 " Williams D.
    126091 " Mason B.
    82173 " Sizeland R.

ATTACHED MEN
    41944 Corporal Rock C.P. (21st. Middlesex)
    281631 L/Cpl. Stewart A. (10/11th.H.L.I.)
    28624 Private Sullivan D. (18th. Welsh)
    61172 " Emsley J. (-do-)
    92822 " Gardner G.R. (Middlesex)
    28446 " Garland M. (18th. Welsh)
    2068 " Baker W. (10/11th.H.L.I.)
    61222 " Jones J.O. (18th. Welsh)
    1077 " Davies W.A. (21st. Middlesex)
    202991 " Pritchard O.T. (18th. Welsh)
    61147 " Coleman H. (-do-)
    28246 " Davies T.C. (-do-)
    61236 " Newton W. (-do-)
    41448 " Mullett W.H. (21st. Middlesex)
    56043 " Perry W. (18th. Welsh)

B Company.
    3261 " Ryan T.
    35256 " Caldwell G.
    40854 " Haughie C.
    30237 " White A.H.
    42598 " Hall J.
    37599 " Reid G.

C Company.
    66224 Sergeant Hepburn J.
    2570 Corporal Root F.
    201946 Private Barnes A.B.
    33904 " Clare J. (13th. Yorks.)
    16890 " Cheetham J. (-do-)
    33851 " Chew H.L. (-do-)
    1368 " Hagger R
    85750 " Johnson W.H.
    82365 " Lowery G.

Casualties continued.   (4)

CASUALTIES   OTHER RANKS.

MISSING continued.

C Company	No 63545	Private	Lawrence	R.
	96530	"	Millbank	W.
	19785	"	Sunley	J. (13th. Yorks)
	23242	"	Sykes	T. (-do-)
	124583	"	Watts	A.J.
	128326	"	McLaren	A.

D Company	60989	Sergeant	Livermore	W.W.
	98942	"	Webster	R.
	44023	Private	Fielder	H.
	20508	"	Manning	W.
	33626	"	Clegg	S.
	55236	"	Brown	J.

MISSING BELIEVED PRISONERS OF WAR.

D Company.	16836	Sergeant	Johnson	W.
	68638	L/Cpl.	Woodward	S.
	29600	Private	Griffiths	S.
	128535	"	Walmsley	T.
	85554	"	Bygrave	C.A.

MISSING BELIEVED KILLED.

| D Company. | 18464 | Sergeant | Page | P. |

40th. BATTALION MACHINE GUN CORPS.

REPORT ON OPERATIONS 21st - 26th. MARCH 1918.

The action of the 40th. Battalion Machine Gun Corps during the recent operations naturally divides into two parts.
(A) Defence of HENIN HILL and HENIN by "A" Company.
(B) Defence of the line from just south of ST LEGER and from NEUVILLERS to the SOUTHERN BOUNDARY of the VI CORPS FRONT. "B", "C" and "D" Companies with "A" Company 59th. Battalion Machine Gun Corps.

"A"

On the 21st March 1918, "A" Company 40th. Battalion Machine Gun Corps, which had been detailed for the close support of the 119th Infantry Brigade was ordered to take up defensive positions on HENIN HILL.

Orders were subsequently received that 4 Guns were to be detached to hold the sunken road WEST of CROISILLES. These 4 guns fought to the last man and the last round but were finally destroyed.

About 3.a.m. on the 22nd MARCH 1918 the 119th Infantry Brigade was ordered to withdraw to HAMELINCOURT its place being taken by the remnants of the 101st. Brigade, 34th. Division. "A" Company 4th. Battalion Machine Gun Corps was ordered to continue to hold HENIN HILL.

About 10.a.m. the enemy attacked the right slope of the Hill advancing in massed formation under cover of the mist. The Infantry commenced to withdraw on the right and finally at about 1.p.m. the hill was evacuated except by the BUFFS on the extreme left and the Machine Guns which were sited along the whole of the crest. These Machine Guns continuously had excellent targets and forced the enemy to withdraw from the SOUTHERN edge of the Hill where he had established a footing.

About 5.30.p.m. under cover of a heavy bombardment the enemy advanced in great strength to the attack of the crest of the hill, moving in "swarms". The seven guns on the right fired throughout doing great execution. Finally however they were completely surrounded by the enemy who had succeeded in working round their right flank. Nevertheless 4 guns succeeded in penetrating the enemy lines and were again brought into action. On the left no frontal attack developed but the two guns here sited under the command of 2nd.Lt.T.F.P.NUNN fired on the enemy as they advanced on both flanks until ordered by the senior Infantry Officer to withdraw to conform with the general British line.

About 4.a.m. on the 23rd MARCH 1918 a withdrawal to HENIN was ordered. Here Lt.NUNN found 2 of the guns previously mentioned which had succeeded in making their way back through the enemy lines. He organized guns into a section, obtained belt boxes from the Guards Brigade and came into action in the 3rd. System astride the NEUVILLE VITASSE ROAD outside HENIN.

During the 23rd MARCH 1918 from 10.a.m. to 2.30.p.m. the enemy continuously attacked in massed formation but although two of his guns had been put out of action, Lt.NUNN succeeded in preventing the enemy from penetrating our wire. A further attack developed later in the day with the same result. The casualties caused to the enemy by these guns were enormous.

During the night of the 23rd. MARCH 1918 the section was withdrawn and rejoined the Battalion under orders issued by VITH. Corps.

The courage and devotion to duty displayed by all ranks of this Company enabled HENIN HILL to be held until nightfall, when the enemy was able to work round the right flank and attack the guns on the SOUTHERN part of the HILL from the rear.

The heaviest casualties were inflicted on the enemy whose repeated attacks in close formation were again and again completely broken up.

(2)

"D"

On 21st MARCH 1918 "D" and "B" Companies were ordered to take up positions in the 3rd system to support 120th and 121st Infantry Brigades. "A" Company of the 39th Battalion Machine Gun Corps was already in Battery Positions along this system. The guns of "D" Company arrived at the ST LEGER-VAULX road at 5 p.m. on the 21st MARCH 1918 and immediately came into action. The left section under 2nd. Lt. THOMAS saw about 600 of the enemy advancing West of MOEUVRE and coming into action from their limbers annihilated them.

A little later B Company took up a line from N'HOMME MORT to the SOUTH of ST LEGER.

The guns were now disposed in depth along the 3rd system, and the night of the 21st/22nd MARCH 1918 passed without much incident.

At about 10 a.m. on the 22nd MARCH 1918, the enemy drove strong attacks along the MOEUVRE VALLEY. 2nd. Lt. SHEPPARD with No.3 section and Lt. ASHBY with 2 guns of No 4 section "D" Company brought heavy fire to bear on them inflicting very heavy casualties and on one occasion annihilating about 1,000 of the enemy in massed formation.

About 2 p.m. the left flank of the 4th Corps was driven in, but the right section of the 39th Battalion under Captain STANLEY and the 6 guns of the 40th Battalion Machine Gun Corps above mentioned remained in position and prevented the envelopment of our right flank.

The Infantry line was now readjusted so as to join on with the IV Corps in R.24.b. and the Machine Guns on the right conformed to this movement after covering the withdrawal of the Infantry.

On the left to the SOUTH EAST of ST LEGER fierce fighting was taking place. Two guns of "D" Company were sent forward to deal with the situation.

The 2 guns came into action with great success and were when our counter-attack was made, able to deal with the retreating enemy.

Two guns were also pushed forward on the extreme right in support of the ARGYLLS as at this point the situation was somewhat obscure. Lt. DAVIS who was in command of these guns was able to assist very materially in the defence of VAULX.

The situation when night fell on the 22nd MARCH 1918, was that our guns were covering the right flank from VAULX to D.15.c. where B Battery of the 39th Battalion Machine Gun Corps was still in action and thence along the 3rd system to the SOUTH of ST LEGER the guns being disposed in a triple line.

During the night of the 22nd MARCH 1918, after consultation with the Brigadier Commanding, the 120th Brigade 6 guns were placed in the Army line to cover the ground in advance of a line between NOREUIL and the Sugar Factory at VAULX. 4 guns from reserve were also placed in the bank at R.28.a. to assist in the defence.

"B" Company supporting the 119th Brigade were now in position behind ST LEGER and in the CROISILLES switch where they remained until the night of the 23rd MARCH 1918, and assisted the defence obtaining numerous targets at long ranges which were most successfully dealt with.

On the night 22nd/23rd MARCH 1918, elements of the enemy penetrated into NOREUIL but were driven out on the morning of the 23rd MARCH 1918 by a counter-attack in which our Machine Guns co-operated destroying the retiring enemy.

SOUTH of NOREUIL the enemy heavily bombarded the Army line at 11 a.m. and 1.35 p.m. and made numerous attacks all of which were dispersed by our Machine Gun fire.

NORTH of NOREUIL the enemy launched a heavy attack in the afternoon and forced our Infantry back towards the Army line. Three sections of Machine Guns caught him as he advanced over the ridge doing great execution, and covering the withdrawal of our Infantry, who formed up somewhat in advance of the Army line.

These guns at about 5 p.m. then took up positions in the sunken road running from NOREUIL to NOREUIL about 6 p.m. the enemy again attacked and forced our Infantry to withdraw to the Army line. The Machine Guns were again able to cover the withdrawal and to inflict very heavy casualties in the Germans. They then withdrew behind the line occupied by the Infantry.

Orders being now received for B Section to move to the to support the 174th Brigade. The Machine Gun Company found was in action and in R.22.c. and there left remnants of the 120th and 121st when lay on the line they held find a reserve completely surrounded by the

(3)

enemy, and after a conference of officers decided to break their way
through to the British Line. Our Machine Guns fired a short bombardment
down each end of the Sunken Road, and the whole party then charged
NORTH through the enemy and succeeded in linking up with our troops
in the Southern outskirts of the village.

On the night 23rd/24th MARCH 1918, a conference of the Machine Gun
Commanders was held at 119th Brigade Headquarters and the Machine Gun
defence co-ordinated.

The line held by Machine Guns now ran round the EAST of ERVILLERS
along the ARMY LINE to the Corps Boundary with a secondary line of
defence just EAST of the BAPAUME-ARRAS Road.

On the 24th MARCH 1918 the enemy made continuous attacks on MORY and
suffered heavy casualties from the fire of Batteries of "C" and "D"
Companies which were able to catch him in enfilade.

On the night 24th/25th MARCH 1918, a withdrawal of our right was
ordered as this flank was in the air.

During this withdrawal the enemy again attacked MORY and succeeded
in establishing himself therein and our line was withdrawn so that it
ran along the EAST of the ARRAS-BAPAUME Road and in front of ERVILLERS.

Strong attacks were now being made on ERVILLERS and our advanced
Sections of Machine Guns were in front of the Infantry line.

2 guns of No 4 Section "C" Company were surrounded and rushed by the
enemy. L/Corporal CROSS succeeded in rejoining the remaining two guns
of his Section.

When day broke, having obtained the permission of Sgt. BRENNAN
commanding the Section, he reconnoitred the position of his captured
guns and found it occupied by the enemy. He attacked them single handed
and captured seven Germans whom he forced to carry back his guns,
tripods and ammunition to our lines where he rejoined his Section.

This Section subsequently was able to destroy a very heavy attack
by the enemy made in 6 waves at a range of from 1,400 - 1,600 yards.

Twelve guns of "C" Company were fighting in advance of our Infantry.
No 3 Section 2nd Lt AMOS which was in a particularly advanced position
fought their guns to the last man.

One gun of No 1 Section "C" Company on the right of ERVILLERS manned
by one man only (CORPORAL DAY) remained in action after the Infantry had
withdrawn and held off the enemy till a counter-attack made by the
MIDDLESEX with elements of LEICESTERS and LINCOLNS re-established the
position. A defensive line consisting of 4 guns of No 1 Section "C"
Company and 2 guns of the 59th Battalion Machine Gun Corps was now
formed to consolidate the position.

On the 25th MARCH 1918 about mid-day the enemy attacks on ERVILLERS
were resumed. No 2 Section (2nd Lt. KENT) who was in position at S.26.b.
was enabled to deal with large masses of the enemy, and to inflict very
heavy casualties on them. This Section only withdrew when it was
practically surrounded when it came into position on the high ground
just EAST of ERVILLERS.

On the night of the 25th/26th MARCH 1918, orders were issued for the
guns of the 40th Battalion Machine Gun Corps to withdraw as the 42nd
Battalion Machine Gun Corps had taken over the Machine Gun defence of
the line.

Lt. ROUTH with No 1 Section "C" Company however voluntarily remained
in the line until he had expended every round of his ammunition,
fighting his guns within 25 yards of the enemy until practically
surrounded.

Then having no more ammunition he successfully extricated his Section
and carried his guns to SAPIGNIES where he had just touch with his limbers.

2nd. Lt. LYONS with No 3 Section "D" Company also volunteered to
remain and fought his guns to the last. This Section was completely
surrounded and there are no survivors.

2nd.Lt. BAKER with No 2 Section "C" Company also remained and only
withdrew about dawn on the 26th MARCH 1918.

2nd.Lt. BURKE "D" Company volunteered to remain and held the
front line with Infantry and 2 Machine Guns of 59th Battalion Machine
Gun Corps until another Officer arrived and took over.

Mention must also be made of Lt. BRITAIN with his 4 guns who
remained in his position after the Infantry had withdrawn and held
the enemy firing at 600 yards range from dense masses. The Infantry
subsequently advanced and took up their position in line with the
Machine Guns.

(4)

"C"

Throughout the operations all ranks fought with the greatest gallantry and tenacity and with absolute disregard of danger.
The enemy attacked in close formations which gave our Machine Guns ideal targets at both long and short ranges. It is difficult to estimate the casualties caused him by our Machine Guns fire but they must have been enormous.
It is impossible to give the names here of all who deserve recognition but I wish to place on record the invaluable services rendered by Major W.C.COOPER, Major D.J.AMERY-PARKES, Major B.C.DAVEY, Captain G.McCRAE, Captain M.G.KEARNEY, all of whom displayed in a marked degree the greatest gallantry and leadership.
The casualties incurred by the Battalion were:-

OFFICERS	Killed	5
	Missing believed Killed	2
	Wounded	3
	Wounded (Gas)	2
	Wounded remained at duty.	1
	Missing	3
OTHER RANKS	Killed	9
	Wounded	65
	Missing	61

"D"

LESSONS LEARNT FROM THE RECENT OPERATIONS.

1. The vital importance of handling the guns by Sections was emphasised. The advantages of such an organisation were as follows:-
   (a) Enemy attacks of vast strength were completely broken up. Less than four guns could not have coped with the situation. Many of these attacks were completely dispersed at ranges of between 1,500 and 2,000 yards.
   (b) The Section Commander has a complete "live" unit under his control which he was able to handle as the situation demanded. Further, flexibility was obtained, as Section could be moved to threatened points which would have been impossible if the guns had been separated.
   (c) Great economy of personnel was effected. Limbers and Pack Mules were of value in this respect. It was largely due to the economy thus effected that casualties incurred were comparitively small.

2. A considerable number of men were detailed as runners and reports sent at frequent intervals to Company Headquarters, whence communication was by telephone and runner to O.C. Battalion (Company Headquarters were with Brigade Headquarters). As a result the Officer Commanding Battalion was in complete touch with the situation throughout. During the day of the 22nd and the nights of the 23/24th and the 24/25th MARCH 1918 the Officer Commanding Battalion visited the line and co-ordinated the defence.

3. During a short period of training preceeding the enemy attack, in addition to the hours spent in Machine Gunnery much time was devoted to Physical and Bayonet Training, Close Order Drill etc. As a result the offensive spirit and discipline of the Battalion was excellent, and it was able to withstand repeated enemy assaults.
Officers during the training period had been very carefully instructed in tactical principles, upon which principles they acted throughout the action with complete success.

26th. March 1918.   Cmdg. 4th. Battalion Machine Gun Corps.

40th Divisional M.G.C.

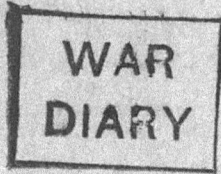

40th BATTALION

MACHINE GUN CORPS

APRIL 1918

Attached :-   Report on Operations 9th-14th
              Lessons learnt.
              Casualties.
              Map.

Vol 3

4.Oth. BATTALION MACHINE GUN CORPS.

WAR DIARY.

APRIL 1918.

Army Form C. 2118.

WAR DIARY
or
INTELLIGENCE SUMMARY.
(*Erase heading not required.*)

Instructions regarding War Diaries and Intelligence Summaries are contained in F.S. Regs., Part II. and the Staff Manual respectively. Title pages will be prepared in manuscript.

Place	Date	Hour	Summary of Events and Information	Remarks and references to Appendices
HAZEBROUCK 5 A.				
SAILLY-SUR-LYS.	1st April		Relief by "B" and "D" Companies of two Companies of 57th Battalion Machine Gun Corps in the line reported complete at 1.30.a.m. Relief by "C" Company of remaining Company of 57th Battalion Machine Gun Corps in the line (centre subsector), and by "A" Company of Company of 57th. Battalion Machine Gun Corps in Reserve at SAILLY SUR LYS.	
CROIX DU BAC	2nd. April		Battalion Headquarters moved to CROIX DU BAC in relief of 57th Battalion Machine Gun Corps, and command of Machine Guns in Sector passed at 10.a.m. Battalion Transport - less Transport of Company in Reserve - moved to PETIT MORTIER.	
	3rd. April		Reconnaissance of Rear System of Machine Guns made by C.O. and reorganized as shewn in Appendix I	
	4th. April		Reconnaissance of Forward System of Machine Guns made by C.O. Fresh positions sited. Congratulatory message received from G.O.C. 40th Division, specially mentioning Major D.J.AMERY PARKES, Major M.C.COOPER, Captain G.McCREE and Captain E.G.HERBERT.	
	5th. April		Further reconnaissance of Forward System of Machine Guns by C.O. Fresh positions sited.	
	6th April		Line reorganized as shewn in attached map (Appendix I.) giving one Machine Gun Group for each Brigade in the line, with Headquarters at BARTLETTE FARM and CANTEEN FARM respectively.	
	7th April		Left Group Headquarters moved to N.21.a.8.2. Three Sections of Company in Reserve at SAILLY SUR-LYS in Corps.Reserve attached to 50th Division. One Section of Company in Reserve remain in Divisional Reserve attached 120th Brigade under orders to move at 30 minutes notice.	CROIX DU BAC
	8th April		Preparations made for support of raid by 21st MIDDLESEX REGIMENT 121st Brigade, to be made at dawn 9th April 1918 by 8 guns, 4 guns from Eight Group and Four Guns from Reserve. Relief of "B" Company by "A" Company, and of "D" Company by "B" Company in Left Sector of Forward System. "D" Company, less one Section retained in the line for raid, move to SAILLY SUR LYS. Three Sections Reserve Company released from Corps Reserve come into Divisional Reserve.	

A7992. Wt. w1859/M1297 750,000. 1/17. D. D & L. Ld. Forms/C2118/4.

WAR DIARY
or
INTELLIGENCE SUMMARY.

(Erase heading not required.)

Army Form C. 2118.

Place	Date	Hour	Summary of Events and Information	Remarks and references to Appendices
HAZEBROUCK 5 A.	9th. April		Enemy launched a heavy attack at dawn after a bombardment commencing at 4.15. a.m. on Portuguese Front and on our Right Brigade Front. Battalion Headquarters moved to DOULIEU at 2.20.p.m. and subsequently to VIEUX BERQUIN. Battalion Transport moved to VIEUX BERQUIN. Three gun limbers remained at DOULIEU.	Operations from 9th-14th April 18. are dealt with in detail in Appendix 2.
	10th. April 11th. April		Major M.C.COOPER placed in temporary command of Infantry covering PETIT MORTIER. Battalion Headquarters and Battalion Transport moved to RUE DE BOIS and subsequently to LA HAUTE LOGE west of HAZEBROUCK. Advanced Headquarters at VIEUX BERQUIN. 40th. Division withdrawn from line.	
LA HAUTE LOGE.	12th. April		Companies commence move to LA HAUTE LOGE. 40th Division take up positions in defence of STRAZEELE BORRE and PRADELLES.	
	13th. April		40th. Division less 40th. Battalion Machine Gun Corps withdrawn from the line. 40th Battalion Machine Gun Corps attached to 31st Division. Forward Machine Gun positions occupied.	
	14th. April		31st. Division withdrawn from the line at 4.a.m. 40th. Battalion Machine Gun Corps attached to 1st Australian Division. Battalion withdrawn from the line during the afternoon and concentrate at LA HAUTE LOGE.	
	15th. April		Battalion moved to MOULLE by march route. No man fell out on the march. Company Commanders Conference. Casualties, reorganization and refitting, the Battle and lessons learnt therein discussed.	
MOULLE	16th April		Work of reorganisation commenced. Battalion proceeded to Baths. Men of Battalion paid. Battalion Canteen opened.	
	17th April		Orders received for formation of a Composite Brigade to include one Company 40th. Battalion Machine Gun Corps.	
	18th April		"D" Composite Company mobilized at 5.p.m. and was inspected by C.O.	

Army Form C. 2118.

WAR DIARY
or
INTELLIGENCE SUMMARY.
(Erase heading not required.)

Instructions regarding War Diaries and Intelligence Summaries are contained in F. S. Regs., Part II. and the Staff Manual respectively. Title pages will be prepared in manuscript.

Place	Date	Hour	Summary of Events and Information	Remarks and references to Appendices
HAZEBROUCK 5.A. MOULLE	19th April		C.O. proceeded in early hours of the morning to take over temporary command of 33rd Battalion. Reorganisation of Battalion proceeded with. C.O. rejoined Battalion in the afternoon.	
	20th April		"A" Composite Company formed under orders of C.O.	
	21st April		"D" Composite Company moved to STAPLE AREA with No.1 Composite Brigade. Battalion -less "D" Company - moved to MORINGHEM.	
MORINGHEM	22nd April		Few remaining men of "B" and "C" Companies attached to "A" Company for training. Training of men recently transferred from Infantry proceeded with.	
	23rd April		"D" Composite Company with No 1 (121st) Composite Brigade moved to RUELD.	
	24th April		Headquarters, "A", "B" and "C" Companies proceed to Baths at MOULLE.	
	25th April		Orders received that 40th Division is to be disbanded.	
	26th April		Breaking up of 40th Division suspended by wire, and order for formation of a second Composite Brigade to include a second Company 40th. Battalion Machine Gun Corps received. No 2 Composite Brigade to be prepared to move at 2.p.m. 27th April 1918. "A" Composite Company, formed on 20th April 1918 ready to move immediately.	
	27th April		Battalion remains at MORINGHEM. Usual training proceeded with. Battalion concert held in Y.M.C.A. PETIT DIFQUES.	
	28th April		"D" Composite Company moved from RUELD AREA to PROVEN AREA. Church Parades at MORINGHEM.	
	29th April		Orders received for Headquarters, "A", "B" and "C" Companies to move to Forward Area 30th. April 1918.	

WAR DIARY
or
INTELLIGENCE SUMMARY.

Army Form C. 2118.

Place	Date	Hour	Summary of Events and Information	Remarks and references to Appendices
HAZEBROUCK 5 A. ST OMER	30th April		C.O. reconnoitres EAST POPERINGHE line with O.C. No 2 Composite Brigade. O.C. "A" and Section officers reconnoitre line. "A", "B" and "C" Companies moved to ST OMER. Battalion Headquarters to ST OMER.	Appendix No 1. Map CROIX DU BAC. 2 Report on Operations. 3 Lessons Learnt. 4 Casualties.

40th. BATTALION MACHINE GUN CORPS.

REPORT ON OPERATIONS 9th - 14th. APRIL 1918.

Reference Map CROIX DU BAC 1/20,000.
HAZEBROUCK 5a. 1/100,000.

The action of the 40.t. Battalion Machine Gun Corps during the operations of the 9th-14th April 1918, naturally divides itself into 4 periods.
(1) The enemy attack of the defensive systems east of the River LYS on April 9th. 1918.
(2) The enemy attacks on the crossings of the River LYS, April 9th and 10th 1918.
(3) The operations in the STREENWERCK Switch and the withdrawal to line running East of LE VERRIER, April 10th, 11th and 12th 1918.
(4) The operations in front of STRAZEELE subsequent to the withdrawal of the remainder of the 40th Division from the line, April 13th and 14th 1918.

The general dispositions of Machine Guns prior to the enemy attack were as follow :-
(a) A forward System of 24 guns sited behind the general line of the River Layes.
(b) A rear System of 16 guns running from WINDY POST in front of FLEURBAIX to CANTEEN FARM.
These guns were organized in two groups — one to each Brigade holding the line. Each group having 4 guns in immediate Reserve.
(c) 16 guns (One Company) and the details of the Battalion some 150 in number in Divisional Reserve at SAILLY SUR LA LYS.

The enmemy after a short but very heavy bombardment commenced at 4.15. a.m. on the 9th instant, attacked the 1st PORTUGUESE DIVISION and our Right Brigade at dawn. He made rapid progress on the Portuguese Front but was held by our forward Infantry Posts till 7.30.a.m. when he began to press back our right flank.

About 9.30.a.m. the enemy succeeded in forcing his way through the Infantry Post near V.C.CORNER and advanced along RUE DELVAS, the RUE PETILLON and the road leading to CROIX BLANCHE.

The three Machine Gun Posts on the right flank of the forward system now found themselves practically surrounded, and with the exception of 1 gun (Cpl.WALLACE) were destroyed after fighting to the last. Cpl.WALLACE however succeeding in rejoining his Company Headquarters with 1 gun and 1 belt box. The further progress of the enemy in this area was however very considerably delayed by the actions of these Machine Gun Posts, while hostile attemps to deploy from the RUE DELVAS was stopped by the guns of B.2. Post in A.32.c. This Post remained in action until 2.p.m. and inflicted very heavy casualties on the enemy before finally every gun was destroyed.

Meanwhile on the extreme right B.1. Machine Gun Post, 4 guns 2nd. Lt. DUNN in N.1.d. near WINDY POST were in action against the enemy who having pressed back the PORTUGUESE were gradually encircling our men. This Section when last heard of was fighting at 1.30.p.m. but was practically surrounded by the enemy.

Meanwhile the 4 Reserve Guns of the Right Brigade were brought into action at FACTORY POST where they were heavily attacked at 1.30.p.m. They succeeded in inflicting heavy losses on the enemy but finally at 4.p.m. were nearly surrounded and under orders of the Infantry Commander fought a rear-guard action covering their retirement with Lewis Guns— taking up positions on the NORTH of SAILLY covering the bridgehead. During this retirement in conjunction with 4 guns of the Reserve Company which had been sent to co-operate with the 2nd .ROYAL SCOTS FUSILIERS they did most effective work at the cross roads in SAILLY whereby the withdrawal of the Infantry to the NORTH BANK of the River was covered and heavy casualties inflicted on the Germans.

At 12 noon hostile forces had penetrated just SOUTH of CROIX BLANCHE and were moving in considerable numbers on BARLETTE FARM. Here Lt.BAIN and 2nd.Lt. ELLIS with the gun brought back by Cpl.WALLACE and with 50 Infantry whom they had collected put up a most determined stand but finally fresh parties of the enemy came into action against them with Light Machine Guns from the rear, and orders being received from the G.O.C. 119th. Infantry Brigade they fell back to YORK POST.

On the left Brigade Front our Machine Guns first came into action about

9.15.a.m. to the right of BOIS GRENNIER and as the enemy attack developed NORTHWARD a defensive flank was formed running along SHAFTESBURY AVENUE towards CANTEEN FARM.

The general situation about 1.30.p.m. 9th instant was that the Forward Machine Gun Posts of the Right Brigade were surrounded but that the enemy was held on the line of our Rear Machine Gun Posts and by our Reserve Sections on the Right flank, but that he was succeeding in working round these from the NORTH WEST.

FLEURBAIX though practically surrounded was still holding out.

During the morning the two remaining sections of the Reserve Company, moved with all the details of the Battalion a total of some 200 men to the RUE DES BRUGES. On their way however they were very heavily shelled and their limbers were hit, the animals killed and several guns destroyed. Nevertheless they came into action about 3.p.m against the enemy and fighting as Infantry they succeeded in greatly delaying his advance, counter-attacking him twice successfully until finally linking up with the Infantry, they were withdrawn to the NORTH Bank of the River LYS.

About 2.30.p.m. a limber Corporal reported to Battalion Headquarters that 2 limbers were near BAC ST MAUR, the animals killed and the limbers partially destroyed by shell fire, Lt. J.G.DUNCAN with a small party of employed men at Headquarters very gallantly succeeded in extricating 5 guns whichn he brought into action to cover the BAC ST MAUR bridgehead, where he was joined by Captaing E.G.HERBERT and Major D.J. AMERY-PARKES, M.G.C., who had been ordered by the G.O.C. 119th Brigade to take command of the troops defending the bridgehead.

The general situation about 5.p.m. therefore was that 11 guns were covering the BRIDGEHEADS across the LYS while 14 Machine Guns were in action on the line held by the Left Brigade running along SHAFTESBURY AVENUE Northwards towards FORT ROMPU., the remaining guns either having been destroyed or being still in action though completely surrounded by the enemy.

2.
DEFENCE OF THE LYS RIVER BRIDGEHEADS.

On the right the Bridgeheads were successfully held throughout the night but on the left the enemy about 5.30.-6.p.m. succeeded in crossing the river about square H.13. and in establishing himself in a farm near the FACTORY in H.13.a.

As a result our line on the left was forced back about dusk behind CROIX DU BAC. A Brigade of the 25th Division then relieved our troops on this flank who concentrated at LE PETIT MORTIER.

On the right at 10.a.m. on the 10th instant the enemy succeeded after a heavy bombardment in crossing the SAILLY BRIDGE after destroying by Shell Fire the Machine Guns and Lewis Guns manned by Machine Gun Corps personnel who were guarding it. The Infantry then withdrew but 2nd. Lieut E.R.HARRIS having found a section of the 50th. Battalion Machine Gun Corps who were without an Officer, fought these guns until all the guns and teams were destroyed.

The situation about noon of the 10th instant was therefore as follows. - Remnants of the 40th Battalion Machine Gun Corps with 9 guns were concentrated at LE PETIT MORTIER, while 11 guns on the left had been linked up with the 34th Division and were co-operating in their gradual withdrawal to conform withnthe general line.

3.
ACTION IN THE STEENWERCK SWITCH AND IN FRONT OF LE VERRIER.

During the 11th and 12th. instant our Machine Guns on the left co-operated with the Infantry and covered them, as under pressure of attacks delivered from the South East they gradually fell back on LE VERRIER, while our guns on the 34th Division Front also fought with the Infantry, who took up a line South East of PONT DE NIEPPE along the railway. On a number of occasions during this period out guns were able to deal most effectively with considerable bodies of the enemy as they massed for the attack.

The guns which had been operating on the front of the 34th. Division were ordered to rejoin the Battalion and this they did at HAZEBROUCK on the 13th instant. While the guns operating on our own front were during the night of the 12th instant concentrated at VIEUX BERQUIN.

4.

OPERATIONS TO THE EAST AND SOUTH EAST OF STRAZEELE.

On the 12th. instant the personnel and guns at VIEUX BERQUIN moved to STRAZEELE where they were reinforced by 7 guns from Battalion Headquarters where new guns had been delivered.

On the afternoon of the 12th instant, under orders of the Division defensive positions were taken up covering HAZEBROUCK from STRAZEELE to AU SOUVERAIN by the above mentioned 12 guns and by 5 additional Vickers from Battalion Headquarters.

On the 13th instant the Battalion came under orders of 92nd Brigade. 12 guns were moved to positions in front of STRAZEELE and 12 guns were detailed to cover STRAZEELE STATION, 6 guns being in Reserve at PRADELLES and 5 at Battalion Headquarters.

The guns EAST of STRAZEELE were not attacked but those covering STRAZEELE-VIEUX BERQUIN ROAD came into action against the enemy who had penetrated on the right and who was exploiting his success with Light Machine Guns. Our guns dealt very effectively with the situations, completely silencing the enemy and enabling our troops to again take up the line.

On the 14th instant orders were received that the Battalion had come under the 1st AUSTRALIAN DIVISION and under instructions given 12 guns were moved to GRAND SEC BOIS.

Later in the day the Battalion was ordered to concentrate and to rejoin the Division. The Battalion concentrated at LA HAUTE LOGE and at 6.a.m. marched to MOULLE.

5.

All ranks displayed great courage and endurance under particularly difficult conditions.

The losses of men and guns are heavy. Heavy casualties were however inficted on the enemy, although on account of his attack being delivered by smaller bodies and on account of poor visibility, these casualties were not so great as those he suffered from our Machine Guns in the operations of the 21st- 25th March 1918.

I desire to bring to notice the names of MAJOR M.C.COOPER, Major D.J. AMERY-PARKES, Major S.C.HASKINS, Captain E.G.HERBERT, Captain P.C.O. BERKELY, Lieut A.M.R.BAIN, Lieut. J.G.DUNCAN and 2nd Lieut. T.E.ELLIS whose gallantry and leadership were beyond all praise.

16th April 1918.   Lieut-Col.
                        Cmdg 40th. Battalion Machine Gun Corps.

40th. BATTALION MACHINE GUN CORPS.

REPORT ON LESSONS LEARNT DURING MARCH AND APRIL 1918.

1. The principle adopted throughout the operations of March and April viz. defence by Machine Gun Posts echeloned in depth was aboundantly justified by results. (vide 1a/48580 Notes on Recent Fighting No.6. T.9.)
These posts should wherever possible consist of a complete section of 4 guns under an officer, and in no case should consist of less

PRELIMINARY REPORT ON THE LESSONS LEARNT DURING THE RECENT OPERATIONS.

(1) In stationary Warfare the main system of Machine Gun Defence should be the rear system for which the Division is responsible.

(2) It is essential that a platoon of Infantry should be attached to each Machine Gun Section as an escort, both in open and in Trench Warfare. Ideally an Infantry Battalion should be affiliated to each Machine Gun Battalion, so that the two may always work together and perfect co-operation be gained. Too much stress cannot be laid on this point.

(3) An improved form of Auxiliary Tripod with increased rigidity is required. Auxiliary Tripods should always be attached to the guns.

(4) Provision of Belt filled S.A.A. is absolutely necessary.

(5) A rigid clip holding 25 or 30 rounds of S.A.A. with carrier should be supplied, so that S.A.A. carried by the Machine gunner can be used for the Vickers gun.

Lieut-Col.
16th. April 1918   Cmdg. 40th. Battalion Machine Gun Corps

with such effect that an attack made on a 1500 yards front in 8 waves advancing in close order was utterly broken up by the time the enemy had reached a line 1400 yards from the gun, the few survivors

40th. BATTALION MACHINE GUN CORPS.

REPORT ON LESSONS LEARNT DURING MARCH AND APRIL 1918.

1. The principle adopted throughout the operations of March and April viz. defence by Machine Gun Posts echeloned in depth was aboundantly justified by results. (vide 1a/48580 Notes on Recent Fighting No.6. T.9.)

   These posts should wherever possible consist of a complete section of 4 guns under an officer, and in no case should consist of less than a subsection (2guns)

   Such a section must not be considered as a Battery which is merely a convenient term used for a number of Machine Guns grouped under an officer for a special purpose, such as harassing or barrage fire, (vide 33192 Part 1, page 7.) but is a complete tactical unit to be handled by its commander as the circumstances dictate for the defence of a definite area.

2. The actual dispositions of such Machine Gun sections are dependant entirely on the nature of the country and the method of enemy attack. Thus in the operations in the vicinity of ERVILLERS and MORY in March, the open country with fields of view up to 2000 yards, and the tremendous massed attacks of the enemy, required the siting of sections so that normally all guns were under the immediate control of the Section Officer, and as a result annihilating fire was brought to bear time after time against massed enemy attacks at long ranges, even when the enemy had succeeded in advancing to ranges of 600 yards and under, the fire of 4 guns was found necessary to break up his advance. So effective did such grouping prove that the enemy casualties were almost incredible

   During the attacks on April 9th however the enemy did not mass his troops in the same numbers although targets of 200-600 men were obtained on some dozen occasions. The nature of the country also necessitated a somewhat wider dispersion of the guns. As the enemy advanced however the ground became more open and as a result our Machine Guns again adopted dispositions closely approximating to those employed at the end of March.

   The principle therefore of utilizing the Machine Gun Section as the fighting unit was entirely vindicated, and experience shows that the junior officers in the corps were sufficiently highly trained to adapt their dispositions to the requirement of the situation, when they had been informed of their role and the general area which they were required to defend.

3. **BARRAGE FIRE**.

   The principle underlying the employment of Machine Guns for barrage fire appears in some instances to have been misunderstood. The ideal of the Machine Gunner as of the Artilleryman must be direct fire on the advancing enemy. Owing however to the necessity for disposition of Machine Guns in depth, rear guns can be used for indirect and concentrated fire with great effect provided that a sufficient supply of S.A.A. is available, while on certain occasions guns on a flank are able even when in advanced positions to fire a most effective enfilade barrage. Such barrage work is however entirely supplementary especially in defensive operations to the main functions i.e. direct fire. Further a barrage to be effective must be thick, a thin barrage is useless.

   An interesting example of valuable barrage fire is furnished by the experiences of C Company of this Battalion during the attacks on MORY on the night 22/23rd March 1918. This Company was occupying positions in advance of ERVILLERS sited primarily for direct fire to the immediate front and to long range direct fire on the ST LEGER-VAULX ridge. It was however able at night to put down a most effective enfilade barrage in front of MORY which was of great value when the S.O.S. was sent up, without in the slightest degree interfering with its essential functions.

   The value also of a Direct Machine Gun barrage must not be forgotten The same Company with 12 guns fired a barrage at enemy seen advancing over the ST LEGER-VAULX ridge at a range of 1800 yards, with such effect that an attack made on a 1500 yards front in 8 waves advancing in close order was utterly broken up by the time the enemy had reached a line 1400 yards from the gun, the few survivors

BARRAGE FIRE continued

finding refuge in a convenient chalk pit.

There is however no possible doubt that all Machine Guns for the defence must be sited primarily with a view to long and visible fields of fire.

4. **PROTECTION OF MACHINE GUN POSTS.**

Whether in trench or open warfare the best protection of Machine gun posts lies in concealment. The placing of Machine Guns in stereotyped strong points is fatal even if shelter is available as the intense concentration of the enemy's artillery fire renders the probability of such guns surviving very small indeed. Loopholed concreted pill boxes are at times of value, but only where it is impossible or very difficult for the enemy to work round in rear of the position.

Machine Guns therefore should as far as possible be sited away from any obvious strong point and all possible care should be taken to conceal their locations. It must however be remembered that when these guns have opened fire further concealment is generally impossible, and the enemy except when he has become hopelessly disorganized proceeds to deal with these posts in two ways.
   (1) By working round the flanks and endeavouring to attack the positions by Light Machine Guns and Infantry, from all directions including the rear.
   (2) By concentration of Artillery and bringing up a forward gun or T.Ms.

There are two ways of countering these actions
   (1) By providing an adequate Infantry defence against the hostile encircling movement.
   (2) Moving the section of Machine Guns.

These two methods must be combined as it is usually very difficult, and sometimes impossible to move the guns unless there is an adequate Infantry escort to protect them.

In as much as Machine Guns during battle are almost invariably in an exposed position the provision of an Infantry escort, as laid down for Artillery (para 105 F.S.R. Pt.1.) is essential.

The experence gained in the recent fighting has proved again and again that Machine Guns are not adequately protected by the distribution of other arms. However carefully in trench warfare the Infantry Posts are disposed in co-ordination with the Machine Gun Posts the former are liable to complete annihilation and communication between them and the Machine Gun Posts breaks down. Once such Infantry Posts are destroyed it becomes merely a question of time before the Machine Gun Posts suffers the same fate, for while such Machine Gun Posts are by day capable of dealing with attacks from the front or forward flanks, they are almost always susceptable to attack from the rear and in any case the advent of night enables the enemy to rush them.

Ideally each Machine Gun Battalion should have an affiliated Infantry Battalion, whose duty is that of escort to the guns, the same platoon co-operating with the same section. This does not mean that the escort is located in the same spot as the guns, but that it is disposed with the sole purpose of protecting the guns from envelopment and destruction, such co-operation would be of equal value in the attack as in the defence as it would enable our Vickers guns to be pushed forward with much more boldness secure in the knowledge that they were adequately protected against surprise.

An example of the value of such bold use of Machine Guns is supplied by the action of a section of A Company of this Battalion SOUTH EAST of STRAZEELE Station. Seeing that the Infantry on their right were being forced to retire by the intense fire of enemy Light Machine Guns which had been pushed forward on the VIEUX-BERQUIN-STRAZEELE Road, The officer commanding this Company advanced two guns to a very forward position and brought concentrated fire to bear on the hostile guns completely silencing them; whereupon the Infantry again took up their original line. This action was as a matter of fact performed without an escort, but a grave risk was taken in thrusting forward these guns which could have been avoided if a platoon of Infantry had been co-operating with the section in question.

(3)

5. <u>CO-OPERATION WITH LEWIS GUNS</u> requires great attention. At the present time the Lewis Gun is a platoon weapon and it is difficult to arrange satisfactory co-operation in Trench Warfare and almost impossible when the fighting has become open. It is suggested that a proportion of the Lewis Guns of a Battalion should be formed into a Lewis Gun Company when co-operation both between Lewis Guns and Vickers Guns, and between the Lewis Guns themselves would be geatly facilitated.

6. <u>RESERVES</u>.
   The provision of adequate Machine Gun Reserves is essential. During both series of operations local Machine Gun Reserves of 1 Sectio to each Brigade Machine Gun Group were provided, both of which Sections proved of the greatest value.
   In addition Divisional and Corps Reserves are also required. At present the limited number of Machine Guns renders the provision of such Reserves only possible at the expense of considerably thinning the forward lines of defence.

7. <u>MAIN MACHINE GUN LINE OF DEFENCE</u>.
   In the operations of the 9th April 1918, the rapid penetration by the enemy of the front of the division on our right enabled him to work round and attack our positions from the rear. Owing to the existence of the local Machine Gun Reserve, above mentioned it was possible to form a defensive flank, but in spite of this fact 14 guns on the right flank were completely surrounded and cut off. The main Machine Gun Line of defence (24 guns) was in this instance sited some 1,000 yards behind the front line, with a second line of 16 guns some 2,500 to 3,000 yards behind the front line. The loss of the above mentioned guns and the involving of the remainder of the forward system rendered control of these forward guns impossible, though the rear line of guns and the Reserves were still for the most part in touch and capable of co-ordinated action.
   The above leads to the conclusion that the main Machine Gun defence of a Division should be sited in the vicinity of the rear line for which a Division is responsible.

8. The question of transport during an action is of great importance. On April 9th 1918 pack animals and limbers were in positions some 4,000 yards behind the line for use of the Sections in immediate Brigade Reserve. All the animals were however in both instances badly gassed, while a large number of the mules of the guns in division -al Reserve were killed by shell fire as they moved forward to their allotted positions.
   During the operations from the 10th - 14th April 1918, when the fighting had assumed a more open character, limbers were found invaluable, and each section took into action its limbers. On one occasion, near STRAZEELE the limbers galloped into action with the Nos 1 and 2 sitting upon them with excellent results.
   A similar case occured on March 21st 1918 near VAULX when a Section of this Battalion came into action from Limbers against 600 advancing enemy at 800 yards range and completely annihilated them.

9. The provision of belt packed S.A.A. is a matter of great urgency. The gradual reduction of the numbers of a section on account of casualties renders belt filling and belt box carrying extremely difficult. Even if teams consist of 8 men it is impossible to carry the full complement of belts, while when teams are reduced to some 3 men a gun, belt boxes have to be discarded in order that the gun, Tripod and Spare Parts may be carried away. The provision of S.A.A.Packed in cheap belts would almost entireley obviate this difficulty.

10. Auxiliary Tripods were found to be of great value and should always be attached to the gun. It would however be an advantage if an auxiliary Tripod with greater rigidity could be designed and manufactured.

23.4.18.   Lieut-Col.
                        Cmdg. 40th. Battalion Machine Gun Corps.

40th. BATTALION MACHINE GUN CORPS.

Casualty Report for Operations from 9th.April 18. to 14th.April 18.

OFFICERS.

KILLED.

A Company.	2nd. Lieut. R.A.BOTHAMLEY	9.4.18.
B Company.	2nd. Lieut. J.B.NORMAN	10.4.18.
C Company.	Captain E.G.HERBERT	9.4.18.
	2nd. Lieut. T.E.ELLIS	10.4.18
D Company.	2nd. Lieut. T.BOWKER	9.4.18.
	Lieut. V.C.LOWRY.	9.4.18.

WOUNDED.

A Company.	Lt. A/Major. D.J.AMERY-PARKES (Middlesex Regt.) seconded M.G.C.	9.4.18.
	Lieut. E.HEMSOLL	9.4.18.
C Company.	Lieut. J.G.DUNCAN (9th.Royal Scots) seconded M.G.C.	9.4.18.
Headquarters.	Lieut. & Q.M. G M.Milnes (Royal Welsh Fusiliers) seconded M.G.C.	9.4.18.

UNACCOUNTED FOR

C Company.	2nd. Lieut. E.L.WILLIAMS	9.4.18.
	2nd. Lieut. W.G.FINCH	9.4.18.

MISSING.

A Company.	2nd. Lieut. C.P.DUNN	9.4.18.
	2nd. Lieut. W.C.WICKHAM	9.4.18.
B Company.	Lieut. J.G.ELMITT	9.4.18.

DIED OF WOUNDS.

D Company.	2nd. Lieut. V.M.DALEY	20.4.18.

40th. BATTALION MACHINE GUN CORPS.

CASUALTY LIST.

OTHER RANKS.

KILLED.

A Company.	No. 131393	Pte.	Syms	P.A.
B Company.	28429	Cpl.	Petrie	W.
	68452	L/Cpl.	Little	W.
	64167	Pte.	Drake	J.
C Company.	68293	Sgt.	Bailey	J.O.
	24275	Pte.	Calver	H.E.
	108457	"	Crow	W.
	126692	"	Mansfield	H.
	54865	"	Gardiner	G.
D Company.	128231	"	Wood	J.

DIED OF WOUNDS.

B Company.	128059	Pte.	Pigg	A.E.
C Company.	35672	Dvr.	Dobson	G.
D Company.	98928	Pte.	Mackay	J.C.

WOUNDED

A Company.	19005	Sgt.	Hunnaball	F.
	13098	"	Booth	H.
	46292	"	Read	B.H.
	29247	Cpl.	Watson	G.L.
	88068	A/Cpl	Winterbottom	S.M.
	117814	"	Scofield	C.H.
	81960	L/Cpl	Kenworthy	H.
	107809	Pte	Baldock	A.H.
	74181	"	Coldham	F.T.
	128721	"	Humphreys	F.
	143447	"	Lewis	W.E.
	4080	"	Martin	J.
	126809	"	Salmon	A.E.
	127195	"	Woods	H.J.
	64256	"	Wylie	W.
	27835	"	Young	W.B.
	44247	"	Nicholls	C.
	28551	"	Hill	S.
	117169	"	Winfield	J.
	97414	"	Curwin	H.
	130997	"	Norris	A.
	143407	"	Bennett	W.H.C.
	74168	"	New	F.
	9463	"	Stevens	A.
	7380	"	Parker	J.H.
	72055	"	Pattison	W.
	131577	"	Thompson	W.
	131800	"	Slee	H.
	8519	"	Peters	A.
Battalion Hd.Qrs.	3102	Cpl.	Platt	F.R.
	45447	Pte	Betts	H.
	54823	"	Arniger	C.F.
	82448	"	Gilles	J.
B Company.	30203	Sgt.	Kefford	B.T.
	7360	Cpl.	Tams	J.
	27902	Pte.	Cook	J.W.
	6471	"	Rust	K.
	63501	"	Tunley	V.
	108796	"	Warren	A.
	97511	"	Thompson	R.
	65624	"	Thompson	A.A.
	58451	"	Skelton	E.W.
	1311668	"	Wicks	F.

(2).

WOUNDED continued.

C Company.

No.	Rank	Name	Initials
36029	C.S.M.	Luck	F.
53291	Sgt.	Blythe	R.
25692	"	Drake	R.S.
29701	"	Orr	H.
29039	L/Cpl.	Treanon	F.
29080	Pte.	Smith	P.
57593	"	Stovold	H.A.
119254	"	Ellis	T.T.
85554	"	Sheldrake	C.R.
126472	"	Norwood	F.C.
29031	"	Goodfellow	P.
85271	"	Brown	S.
143438	"	Crawford	P.L.
74156	"	Welsh	J.
74175	"	Houston	J.
37069	"	Johnstone	G.L.
74174	"	Cook	C.
29038	L/Cpl	Curran	J.
119207	Pte.	Anderson	J.
129409	"	Evans	A.
99189	"	Walker	W. (Shell-shock).
70752	"	Wilding	G.
22313	Sgt.	Emptage	C.G.

D Company.

No.	Rank	Name	Initials
64648	C.S.M.	Miller	H.
98930	Cpl.	McNeish	J.
103273	L/Cpl	Johnston	H.
91954	Pte.	Allton	S.
121642	"	Clements	G.
143460	"	Cocksedge	A.
121671	"	Denton	R.
143451	"	George	A.
97987	"	Hillyard	W.
120297	"	Kersey	W.H.
131856	"	March	W.
88016	"	Grindell	A.
34376	"	Vine	S.P.
104679	"	Wales	C.W.
115470	"	Reid	G.
128354	"	Thompson	J.J.
18815	"	Taylor	C.J.
123185	"	Turnbull	G.H.
53347	"	Towle	R.F.
102083	"	Challen	C (At Duty).

WOUNDED GASSED

B Company.

No.	Rank	Name	Initials
27707	Pte.	Wildey	B.
29042	"	Lambert	J.

C Company.

No.	Rank	Name	Initials
31382	"	Doran	J.
86267	"	Andrews	F.W.
107607	"	Robertson	T.

D Company.

No.	Rank	Name	Initials
85599	"	Bramley	A.

WOUNDED AND MISSING

A Company.

No.	Rank	Name	Initials
43741	B/Cpl.	Curlewiss	A.C.
84170	Pte.	Burr	W.

MISSING.

A Company.

No.	Rank	Name	Initials
9919	Cpl.	Beaumon	P.
20703	Sgt.	Nassan	F.
29172	Cpl.	Spicer	A.
72902	Pte.	Holbrook	J.
85748	"	Higginson	A.
85747	"	Hope	J.
72903	"	Jackson	W.
143406	"	Lay	G.

MISSING continued

A Company

No.	Rank	Name	
119241	Pte.	Parker	S.
143413	"	Perring	C.
118846	"	Selway	E.A.
90498	"	Tinkler	W.
143448	"	Davies	S.
29063	A/Cpl	Lansdown	T.
74126	"	Aylesbury	R.
85429	Pte	Hooper	A.J.
64683	"	Wild	E.L.
74128	"	McFee	J.
117818	"	Corfield	J.
5274	"	Johnson	E.
72909	"	Nunn	C.
126021	"	Ringerse	A.E.127194
127194	"	Wayland	W.
74182	"	Kingham	J.H.
143408	"	Powell	C.A.
99862	"	Reece	
126199	"	Sawyers	A.
36587	"	Willis	C.A.
70552	"	Quinn	W.
128776	"	Ward	S.R.
131903	"	Saunders	T.
127171	"	Martins	C.E.
127501	"	Lloyd	E.J.
117103	"	Robertson	J.
131776	"	Lawrinson	C.
131775	"	Layton	T.E.
131771	"	Lenn	H.
131899	"	Slade	A.W.
131897	"	Southam	G.
131810	"	Treeton	A.C.

B Company.

No.	Rank	Name	
28471	Sgt.	Foggs	J.J.
34450	L/Cpl.	Ives	G.
14327	"	Kirkham	W.
143465	Pte	Creighton	H.
28449	"	Donaldson	G.W.
64257	"	Garstrong	W.
88173	"	Howarth	H.
82699	"	Halpin	T.
7719	"	Jones	W.
74193	"	Jones	T.
63540	"	Lester	R.
52638	"	Lloyd	W.
7882	"	Lund	E.
103266	"	Lees	A.
55689	"	Lines	J.
126919	"	Parker	H.
122078	"	Trumble	W.
29254	"	Woodhouse	J.
16125	"	Scott	J.
64233	"	Wyles	G.
74194	"	Wyatt	G.
143488	"	Watson	R.
25731	"	Younger	W.
98483	"	Smithson	A.E.

C Company.

No.	Rank	Name	
60407	Sgt	Powell	W.H.
118151	Cpl.	Stewart	G.E.R.
29012	L/Cpl	Qualey	T.
5959	Pte	Pumfrey	
204532	"	Muddle	R.E.
14366	"	Crawford	J.
33731	"	Treen	P.
27695	"	Duck	J.
143432	"	Little	F.C.
25689	"	Oakerbee	H.
128041	"	McCawley	J.
125588	"	Humphreys	J.
32814	"	Woodage	H.

MISSING continued

Company	No.	Rank	Name	
C Company.	25706	Pte.	Hobbs	T.B.
	68630	"	Dyde	A.
	143504	"	Norris	A.
	10038	"	Killender	J.
	45276	"	Young	J.
	57691	"	Jackson	A.
	143423	"	Cowin	J.J.
	59136	"	Morris	J.
	31397	"	Tate	R.H.
	60603	"	Cottier	J.H.
	130815	"	Davies	J.A.
	10892	"	Ludgate	G.S.
	128956	"	Little	B.
	143433	"	Harrington	G.
	128277	"	Manton	J.
	30458	"	Bettridge	G.C.
	125122	"	Summerford	E.
	148500	"	Cordell	W.
	70554	"	Tromans	S.
	131313	"	Redgrave	D.
	4911	"	Taylor	W.
	27246	"	Reid	C.
	6094	"	Shimmin	W.
	132459	"	Thomas	W.
	132296	"	Elphick	J.
D Company.	83050	L/Cpl	Aldons	H.H.
	74152	Pte	Carter	A.E.
	123130	"	Dann	T.C.
	30593	"	Dunn	T.
	143452	"	Edwards	A.
	102038	"	Hackett	H.R.
	74133	"	Kells	W.P.
	143453	"	Komlosy	F.
	131410	"	Beaton	J.
	127070	"	Minter	F.W.
	124043	"	Nash	N.J.
	127346	"	Senior	H.
	97615	"	Thompson	G. (Woundedamended)
	131011	"	Postlewaite	W.H.

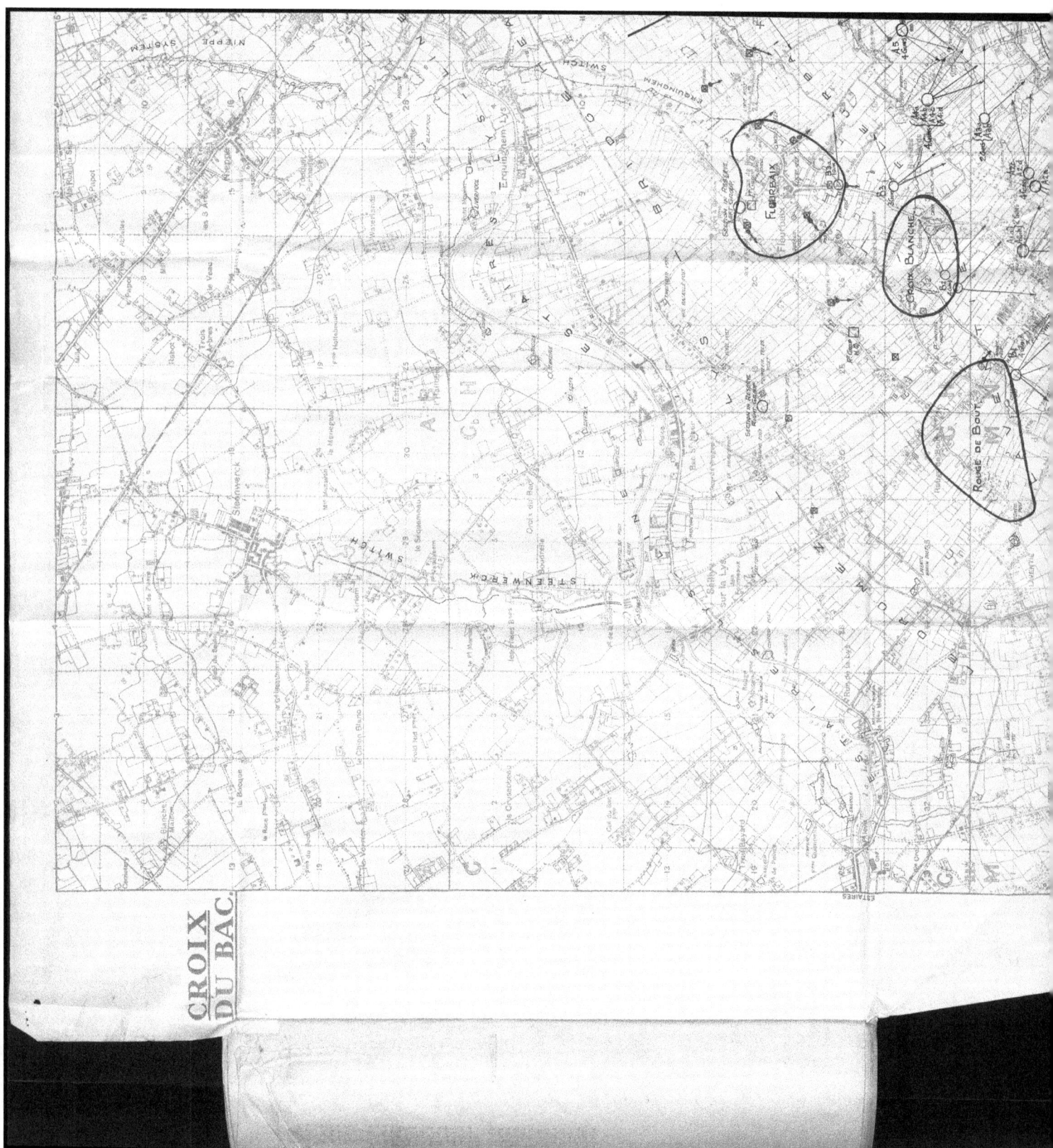

Vol 4

4 Oth. BATTALION MACHINE GUN CORPS.

WAR DIARY

FOR MONTH OF MAY 1918.

Army Form C. 2118.

WAR DIARY
or
INTELLIGENCE SUMMARY.
(Erase heading not required.)

Instructions regarding War Diaries and Intelligence Summaries are contained in F. S. Regs., Part II. and the Staff Manual respectively. Title pages will be prepared in manuscript.

Place	Date 1918.	Hour	Summary of Events and Information	Remarks and references to Appendices
HAZEBROUCK ST OMER.	1st May.		"A" Composite Company, Headquarters and details of "B" and "C" Companies and details of Battalion Headquarters moved to RYVELD.	
	2nd May.		Suspension of breaking up of Division cancelled. "A" Composite Company, and Headquarters "A" and "B" Companies and details attached moved to ZUDROVE. "D" Composite Company moved to RYVELD area.	
	3rd. May.		Stores and equipment of Battalion Headquarters, "A", "B" and "C" Companies handed in to D.A.D.O.S. "D" Composite Company moved to ST MOMELIN area.	
	4th. May.		"A" Composite Company, Headquarters "B" and "C" Companies, and details attached less Transport personnel entrained at WATTEN STATION at 2.30.p.m. Divisional Commander visited WATTEN STATION and addressed Officers and men. "D" Composite Company attend ceremonial Parade at which Divisional Commander distributed decorations. All 40th Battalion Machine Gun Corps recipients present with unit attend, recipients given in Appendix 1. "D" Composite Companys Stores and equipment handed to D.A.D.O.S.	
	5th. May.		Battalion Transport concentrated at ZUDROVE at 9.30.a.m. and proceeded by maron route to ETAPLES staging at BAYEGHAM and DESVRES ; four riders and wheel animals only proceeded, Riders Spare and lead animals remain at ZUDROVE. "D" Composite Company entrained at WATTEN STATION for CAMIERS at 2.30.p.m.	
	6th May.		Disposal of spare and wheel animals to units proceeded with.	
	7th May.		Disposal of animals proceeded with.	
	8th May.		Disposal of all animals except four riders attached Battalion Headquarters completed.	
	9th May.		Under orders received from 40th Division all remaining personnel of 40th Battalion Machine Gun Corps, less skeleton Headquarters entrained at ST OMER for CAMIERS at 2.30.p.m. Orders received that all personnel with exception of Lt.Col. H.G.V.ROBERTS, Major M.C.COOPER, two batmen and two grooms will proceed to CAMIERS on 10th May 1918.	
	10th May.		Major P.C.O.BERKELEY and seven other ranks proceed to CAMIERS with Battalion Records to-day.	

www.ingramcontent.com/pod-product-compliance
Lightning Source LLC
Chambersburg PA
CBHW081248170426
43191CB00037B/2076